SCHIZOPHRENIA
MY CLASSIC
DELUSIONS

By Robert Francis, LCSW

TABLE OF CONTENTS

My message for others who have schizophrenia:

"Do not unnecessarily limit yourself based on the diagnosis of schizophrenia. You are larger than its render. You are larger than its problem. According to each symptom, solutions abide! Let our generation, yours, and mine, be the generation that routinely evidences the global status of recovery as we pave new roads with a golden hope for those who will follow. Do not shy from life because of schizophrenia. Solve its dilemma, forget the rest, and try to achieve with each passing day. In all its varied forms, may you find your solace and an abiding sense of recovery.

You can do it! I know you can!"

FOREWORD

Jan Dirk Blom, MD, PhD, Clinical Psychiatrist and Professor of

Clinical Psychopathology

Look no further. This is the book you have been looking for. Of all the works that have been written on schizophrenia, this is the book that you should read. That is, if you want to gain an impression of what it is about and how it affects one percent of all people world-wide. Not that any two people given this diagnosis are ever the same, but a more powerful account will be hard to find.

I have been following Robert Francis ever since his 2019 debut On Conquering Schizophrenia, I have always been impressed with the way he puts his idiosyncratic experiences and professional reflections into words.

In this, his most personal book yet, he invites us into a time capsule hurtling us back into his twenties when he was on and off medication and floridly psychotic in between. The titular tales are psychopathological as well as literary gems.

Would you ever have guessed that the Marriott is the best place to hide when you are plagued by the delusional terror of paranoia, as we learn in Chapter 1? And, as explained by him in Chapter 6, that poem may be the best place to hide your soul? Yes, your soul.

Psychiatrists have knowledge of the mind and body, but Francis knows that he also has a soul, and he even knows where to put it in times of apparent danger.

Among the eight psychotic episodes rendered here in exquisite detail, my personal favorite is Chapter 3, in which the Supreme Being brings an ode to legendary guitar player Jimi Hendrix. It is proof that Francis has the rarest of gifts: to describe with apollonian clarity - and distance and humor - the dionysian depths of psychotic experience.

What Francis shows us in his book is what we all need to learn: that the past is gone and can touch us no longer - except by bringing enlightenment to ourselves and others. It is in this vein that he recounts his younger self's surreal experiences, lays them out before our astonished eyes, and explains with singular precision and grace what they meant to him then and what they mean to him now.

Reading his exceptional accounts, a comparison that sprung to my mind is the 1988 book entitled Ver Heen (Far Gone) by the Dutch psychiatrist Piet Kuiper, who very nearly succumbed to major depressive disorder, only recovering after an endless struggle, and then putting pen to paper to reflect on his experiences. In Francis' case, the result is a rare glimpse of the architecture of psychosis, in all its frenzy and sometimes mesmerizing beauty.

Another title for this book might therefore have been Rare Insights into Psychosis by a Contemporary Sage. But let's not quibble about words with Robert Francis. He is the master here in each and every respect. Let him have the title and let us be grateful that we have his magnificent book.

Leiden, April 2024

CHAPTER 1
MY NIGHT AT THE MARRIOTT

Together we arrive in my early twenties amid my first onset of psychosis, untreated at that. Chronologically, I would be, approximately, 23 years old and about six months into my first experiences with psychosis. My psychosis grew incrementally, from the once subtle to the then florid. During this episode, I was now florid. I had zero insight into my schizophrenia and had yet been diagnosed. This episode humorously entertains me to this day! (That is, in capable retrospect!)

I lived on the second floor of a two-family house, surrounded by neighbors as you would find in a typical urban city. In this particular episode, auditory hallucinations and associated delusions were running their spirited course. It is a funny thing. Sometimes I have been asked by those close to me who are familiar with my schizophrenia (paranoid type) diagnosis if I recall my episodic psychoses. The easy answer is "yes." In fact, psychosis can be so entirely trying (and almost I think traumatic), I think it etches in my memory banks more so than ordinary or mundane memories. Regarding my psychosis, I often times remember well, and with great detail too.

Together we transport circa 1994 into my kitchen, spacious at that with blue, red, and gray flecked linoleum tile. I am amid an acute psychosis. Remember, psychosis is defined as a breach from reality. Psychosis is the term used in a specified conglomeration of diagnostic symptoms. Psychosis is the prevailing generalized clinical term whereas the admixture of symptoms is specified to the greater general.

Here in my kitchen, I am floridly psychotic. "Florid" is the clinical term for "very" and oftentimes used as a clinical descriptor of psychosis. I have recollection of my stature while standing in my kitchen. I am hearing voices, and they are contributing to my prescient and present delusional status. A "delusion" is a clinical term for a "false belief" i.e., a belief without the requisite reality-based evidence. There are many subtypes of delusions (including paranoid, persecutory, and bizarre among others). I am hearing voices and vociferously. Who are the voices I hear? My surrounding neighbors of course!

Now please do not misconstrue. I am in my home, and they are in theirs. Undeniably, and in no manner logistically possible, audible vocalizations from neighbors in their locale and mine and mine, be heard. I am abundantly hallucinating. I am hearing my neighbors' voices in my head.

This is clinically referred to as "auditory hallucinations" and are abbreviated often as "AH." Auditory hallucinations are a typical hallmark in schizophrenia, and on this particular evening, mine are loud, verace, and also commanding. "Command auditory hallucinations" are a subtype to the general of auditory hallucinations. Command type auditory hallucinations can be of an extremely perilous sort because they are directive to the experiencing individual. When someone is experiencing command auditory hallucinations, the voices are directing, or commanding, the individual to act in some manner. Depending on the correlated command, peril may lurk; be it, a possible directive to hurt oneself or hurt another.

Another subtype of auditory hallucinations is known as "persecutory." Persecutory auditory hallucinations are voices which denigrate or persecute the affected individual. Generally speaking,

4

persecutory hallucinations leave the individual feeling downtrodden, very unwanted, forlorn, and especially isolated.

My auditory hallucinations take the admixtures of a command type along with a persecutory type. As I further share the contents of this episode, the two subtypes will reveal and be apparent.

I hear voices from two separate households. One voice is coming from my right-side neighbor and the other from my backyard neighbor. I perceive them to be speaking with each other, as well as me, and they are in collusion. What is it they are yelling at me about? The voices are telling me I am a most unwanted neighbor. The voices are saying they do not want me around. The voices are persistent.

I think to myself,

"What have I done to offend or warrant? What have I done to deserve such scorn?"

In fact, allow me to add, other than a casual sighting of my neighbors, I know them not from Adam. Further, we have never had a conversation. I would see them on occasion and that was the actual depth of our relationship.

The voices from my neighbors play out like an act in my mind. It's a three-way "conversation" including my own vested discourse. I am nested in my kitchen amid the belief that I am "talking" in a three-way conversation with my neighbors who are void of my kitchen! The conversation is perceived as verace and as an ordinary face-to-face. In addition to the auditory hallucinations, I am also amid the delusional belief known as "mind reading." Mind reading is the delusion of a belief in mind-to-mind communication without need for spoken word. Once

5

of this delusion, one also believes one can communicate mind-to-mind with others across vast geographies.

For example, I can mind-to-mind communicate while in New York City with another in Paris. As such, this symptom communion qualifies as my clinical amalgam i.e., command and persecutory auditory hallucinations amid a mind-to-mind communication delusion.

The voices harken and persist.

After hours of being denigrated and persecuted, then follows the meat to the bone on this episodic delusion. I hear the two voices from the two neighbors, one from my east and one from my south. After some thirty minutes of the voices telling me I am not wanted as a neighbor, not wanted in the neighborhood, and just plain 'ol not wanted in the general, the voices turn colder and shrewder and bite even further. I hear my southerly neighbor exclaim for me to "Get out!." I hear this command several times. I feel entirely denigrated and now I am fearful for my safety. I am beside myself, as geographically beside my neighbors. I still cannot comprehend as to "Why?" this is all happening as I feel I am a decent person.

After repeatedly hearing "Get out!" I develop a plan. I began to pack my car full of my belongings. I have decided to indeed comply and move out. As I packed, I panicked and worried about my safety. I hurriedly pack my car, full to the hilt of my most important belongings. I have decided I am moving out and moving on. I have the notion if I move out I can find another place to live where I can be safe and not harassed. You have to get the visual in your mind because its situation, in long retrospect now, is entirely hilarious. I hurry back-and-forth to my car in my driveway. Amid my hurry, I continue to hear "Get out!"

Maybe ten trips ensue to and fro in total. My car is now full to the top. I jump in my car, and I take off.

You may wonder, where did I go? When amid a delusional terror and fleeing for one's life, allow me to recommend the Marriott!

I drove to a neighboring town and checked myself into the posh hotel. I figured to myself a little pampering was indeed requisite. Because my car was packed full, I parked in an inconspicuous location, checked in, went to my room, and exhaled.

My next move, of course, was to head to the hot tub and pool. I indeed had a most splendid evening at the Marriott! While in bubbles, I made my next day's action plan which entailed scoping out a new apartment proximate to the Marriott.

Prior to my bedding for the evening, I called my grandmother. I wanted her to know, and to tell my mother, regarding my now empty nest and my residence at the Marriott. When I explained in brief the recent series of events, of course, she was most perplexed. She phoned my mother and mom then phoned me.

Mom then did what good moms do. Confused at my erratic behavior, she empathized and was most adamant of me being misconstrued. She reassured me of my obvious and apparent nonsense, and she supported me in my return to my apartment. Her persuasion was well enough for me to return. At this point, based on repetitions of my erratic behavior, my mental illness was becoming clearer and more obvious to those around me.

Nevertheless, please heed my advice. If you ever feel compelled to flee, the Marriott is a terrific landing space. Amid the hot tub bubbles, it's a suitable place to gather your thoughts while planning your next move. I found my night at the Marriott a terrific salve. I attest, you can't make this stuff up.

To this day, I endorse the Marriott luxury. It was a wonderful respite!

I find this episode, like that of my others, in my retrospect, a most amusing sort of tale and craziness. I admonish you, too, to soak in the humorous timbre. In this case, fact is stranger than fiction, and funnier too!

CHAPTER 2
MY CAVORTING WITH FAME

Do you know I cavorted amid the famous?

Before we get to my delusions about my relations with the famous, allow me to provide an initial disclaimer. In no way, manners, or according to the most remote possibility did I ever truly know or interact with those I will mention. It was all complete delusion and florid psychosis. Those I mention do not know that I exist. In reality, it was entirely fictional although, conversely, entirely nonfiction to my then intellect.

We together again take our time machine capsule back to my mid 20's now amid florid psychosis. At this time in my mental health treatment, I was prescribed a healthy dose of Zyprexa, but I was not taking it. I was in a sort of denial that I needed it, although I am sure such a need was becoming obvious to others. By manner of our mutual time machine travel, we arrive at my rented urban apartment. I am floridly psychotic and medication non-compliant.

When you have untreated schizophrenia, or a burgeoning psychosis, the TV really is a most fascinating device. In my instance, and I have read the same for many others, the TV can be a powerful medium. Amid my delusions, the TV became a binary communication device i.e. I believed myself entirely capable of communication with those on the TV, that is, if I gained their potential interest.

Each and every time the TV was on, I believed I was in a two-way communication with those in the TV square. Of course, this sense of communication is entirely unfounded and is indicated by the clinical delusional subtype known as "mind reading."

Mind reading entails the delusional belief that communication is possible, mind-to-mind, without need for verbalization and with inherence across vast geography. This being the case, the images on TV provide ripe opportunity for this delusion to flourish. And flourish it did!

I believed, on a nightly basis, my presence was evident to all on "The Tonight Show with Jay Leno." I would watch and Jay knew I was present along with the viewing audience. For a duration, I thought I was his sidekick like the olden days of McMahon to Carson. I believed that I was communicating with Jay, and all his guests, each time I viewed. I "met" many a star! This delusion persisted for months.

Additionally, similarly via the TV, here is another such experienced delusion. At once, Jerry Lewis used to conduct an annual Muscular Dystrophy telethon. What an amazing venture this was for so many years! Guess what? Yes, I believed myself participating in his telethon during this specific year.

This delusion was verace. While viewing the telethon I was listening to some CDs (if you don't remember what a CD is I wish you well in your longevity!). With the music on in the background, suddenly I believed I was the inherent DJ, or musical provider, to the telethon including as its persistent lowly heard background musical support. I spent hours that day watching the telethon. I believed each CD I chose was the actual background music to the telethon. I spent six hours playing different CDs as the believed musical backdrop. Sometimes, I got applause and admired for my keen selection. This delusion was mostly benign and syntonic.

I thought I was the DJ.

10

I spent all day occupied with watching the telethon and spinning the discs. This experience was entirely propped by the active delusion of mind-to-mind communication. And yes, my efforts were fruitful because we met the telethon goal. As an aside, Jerry Lewis was an amazing charity. Genuinely great, splendid work by Jerry!

Supported by the telepathic delusional belief and egged on by access to TV and its Hollywood stars, I had perceived dalliances with the famous. For example, I had an afternoon with Madonna, regular communication with political figures, occupancy with Oprah, and routine contact with those on my local TV newscasts. I knew them all and interacted with them all. How such a belief coalesces and activates is a personal fascination! The mind-to-mind misapprehension is quite common to us with schizophrenia.

The unwelcome news, in this instance and relative to my delusion, is that it started with frivolity but persisted and culminated amid persecutory belief. Such interactions morphed into a form of personal persecution. My interactions and dalliances soured and abundantly so. Once soured, I could not stop such interactions inherent to my deliberate intent. The persecutory beliefs then cultivated with a blossoming paranoia and an ample psychosis was flourishing.

Of course, the remediation to such a delusion may seem obvious. That is, one cannot communicate mind-to-mind across geography and the TV simply is not a binary communication appliance. The amazing part regarding this delusional episode is how it came to be in a phenomenological sense. I now know the constituents and particulars as to how such a bizarre life experience occurred.

I was having auditory hallucinations; I was hearing voices particularly as seemingly sourced from the external environment. Once the voices began, and since I was hearing voices when no one else was around, by matter of my logic, I deduced I too broadcast my internal voice to others. Once this belief grew by veracity and intensity, I dwelled amid the experience of a capable telepathic communication. Once believing I could communicate in this manner, again in a logical manner, the TV provided me with a looking glass to the world and I could communicate with the famous via its medium. The quick to follow persecutory content was a natural happenstance of believing I was being intrusive to the stars, as an unwanted and heralded marginalized voice with no business instigating such privileged communication.

On a few occasions, when I believed I was directly communicating with those on TV, I then learned that the TV program I was interacting with, inclusive with its inherent stars, was actually not a live program and was taped and previously recorded. Upon this personal recognition, my delusional theory and gestalt folded like a house of cards. I thought to myself, "If it's taped, I can't communicate with them," in a live and spontaneous manner in which I previously thought. Also, the others cannot be communicating with me, as I had perceived, if the program was indeed taped. Outrageously, it took this recognition for the TV delusion to retreat.

I nevertheless maintained a belief in the greater global delusion of mind-to-mind communication, but I was now broken of its veracity and specificity via the TV medium, that is, at least minimally and in a sense. The TV retreated some as my opponent although live TV continued to capture my attention including local broadcasts and live sporting events. My respite came, I believed, when viewing programs taped and not live. In fact, when I watched TV this was my first discernment. Is it live or taped? Do I want to engage in a live event, or do I want the mundane of the taped show? The veracity of this episodic misconstruction shined like a beacon and light.

I was totally persuaded and had no doubts!

When I reflect on this episode, and its inherent conversations and interactions with the famous on the other side of the TV, I now convincingly and knowingly roll my eyes to myself and laugh and scoff.

I tell you, when amid such delusions, I convincingly had some fascinating (and terrifying) interactions with many of the famous. With some gray now in my beard, I now know no one who walks this Earth especially impresses, but at the time I was young and enraptured by fame. Of course, we all put on our pants similarly. But then, at times, it was exciting. This whole fallacious scenario played out over six months, I would estimate, and it then dissipated and morphed in favor of other psychotic episodes.

Did I ever tell you of the time regarding the delusion I call "God's Ode to Jimi Hendrix?" Well, indeed, let us move on with a most vigorous spirit to God and Jimi.

You're not going to believe this next episode!

CHAPTER 3
GOD'S ODE TO JIMI HENDRIX!

Allow me to introduce three items before we grind our teeth into the content of this next episode.

If you are unfamiliar with Jimi Hendrix, I suggest he is a 1960's rock legend and a guitar master of masters. Jimi could rock a guitar like no one else and he was seminal too in his style. Once, Jimi famously set his guitar on fire after a series of sublime riffs! Jimi could ablaze the house on fire with his extraordinary musical talent. If you know Jimi already, I know you will nod in accordance. One of Jimi's most famous songs was titled "Purple Haze." We will return to this title once we traverse into our newest delusion. Jimi, most unfortunately, died at the tender age of 27. He is a member of the Rock 'n' Roll Hall of Fame.

You may wonder why God is playing ode to Jimi Hendrix and not Jimi to God. This is an understandable stance; but, for the time being, allow me a small space for grace.

Lastly, this will be my first documenting specific content involving "God." Please know, I carry no assumptions whatsoever regarding your divine beliefs and further yours are yours and I carry no qualms. Interestingly, I did not choose to have delusional ideations involving God. They simply occurred. Further, my global beliefs involving God have no baring when referencing my religious episodes with God content. In my eye, these are two distinct issues i.e., they are two issues and not one.

My happenstance global beliefs about God, in this context, I offer as irrelevant. I simply want to share such episodic delusions and God happens to fulfill content. Enough said regarding this, I am sure you agree.

I am now age 25. During this period, I was again amid a blossoming and flourishing psychosis, and I was unmedicated and not in treatment. You may find it interesting of my vocation while amid this next unbelievable and ultimately hysterical episodic delusion. Of all the vocational hats to wear, at this time, I was working as a telemarketer. What a general and fascinating vocational escapade was telemarketing including for an estimated six months in total.

As a telemarketer, I was selling charitable contributions to police run organizations. Now, I do not want to explore the ethics of telemarketing, rather I offer, I was doing this work for two reasons and two reasons solely.

One, I needed a dollar. Two, it was an easy hire to acquire. The setting for this next episodic delusion is a medium sized open room with computers lodged with headsets facing all four walls. In total, I estimate, somewhere around twenty of us altogether occupied. The supervisor sat at the head of the room to monitor the goings-on. The computer would dial the number and the sales pitch would ensue.

The day began inconspicuously enough. I entered the vocational forum rational but otherwise ended the day amid my self-titled delusion "An Ode to Jimi Hendrix!" When now reflecting on this, I must say this day was a most turbulent and memorable ride. And for a short duration, this delusion ended me in ample hysteric.

Innocently enough, I began the day at work as I always did, that is, on the phone doing my sales pitch. But this day turned quite wild and did so furiously and quickly. As I began making my calls, I suddenly became preoccupied with my right hand. It didn't look usual to me, and it seemed bonier, elderly, and veinous. I chalked it up to an acute perceptive weirdness. But its weirdness to my eye persisted, and I was preoccupied by its appearance. Then the voice of God, via an auditory hallucination status, entered my perceptive anomaly. God informed me that my hand was in fact the hand of his son, Jesus.

I thought "What?" Followed by "I'm your son, Jesus?"
God confirmed; indeed, I was his son, Jesus.

I continued to make my phone calls but the immediate surroundings, along with my coworkers, began to absorb my attention more than the process of making calls. Moving then further beyond the singular ideation of being Jesus, then came more of a delusional pile-on, that is, according to my perceptions. Suddenly, one of my female coworkers morphed, according to my perception, from a female coworker to the Virgin Mary i.e., the mother to Jesus. I was thoroughly convinced she was Mary! She had a divine sort of glow and further her physical appearance suddenly had a great resemblance to Mary. I scoped further. Suddenly, the entire environment appeared laden with religious figures. All my coworkers appeared as various religious figures including Joseph (Mary's husband), groupings of apostles and prophets, and the supervisor revealed to me as God himself! The entire workplace was chock-full of religious figures.

I remember these perceptions to this day, and they were ultra-verace. There was a uniqueness to my perceptions then. They seemed grandly surreal. For a moment, it all then became amusing to my senses given this novel predicament. I thought my supervisor was God

16

incarnate and all my coworkers were various religious figures. All of this occurred while making mundane sales pitches in a mundane office environment. Then, further, creeped in some paranoia.

The religious ideations persisted but suddenly I was paranoid about telling those on the phone during my sales calls my real name. I thought if they knew my name they would ably gossip and make me a worldwide known entity (which I heartily wanted no part!). I thought if others knew my name they, like was done to Jesus, would instigate a global persecution. I was paranoid that others were now full of malevolent intent.

Amid all this mental chaos, I continue to make phone calls but telling those my name, as was required in the sales script, I began making names up and random names at that. Nothing obtrusive, but not my own. After using a few made up names, my boss called me into his desk to inquire why I was fabricating. I made up a sort of excuse. He didn't acquiesce to my lame excuse, and he reprimanded me and directed me to knock it off. I now can say, that surely was a rational enough directive!

I returned to my call station, and you guessed it, due to my enormous paranoia and feelings of intense vulnerability, I continued with the name fabrications. My boss must have been absolutely flabbergasted and befuddled by my behavior. In fact, additionally, he was most displeased. He called me to his desk again and abruptly fired me on the spot! Honestly, at the acute time, I could not have cared less. With all the chaos in my mind, the firing did not even register as a blip on my radar. I think a typical reaction would at least register as discouragement, but for me on this very peculiar day, I said,

"OK, no problem, I'll see you later!" And I walked out of the office onto the street.

I routinely took public bus transportation to and from employment, and so, I descended to the street and walked to the bus stop to get my ride home. I remember waiting for the bus. It was a beautiful day, according to the weather, and I remember enjoying its pleasantness.

I was fired abruptly and firmly so! I tell you, again, it was entirely a non-issue to my intellect then. In fact, I felt better after the loss!

Believe me, I was abundantly otherwise cognitively occupied. I had larger metaphysical and spiritual occupations to worry about than my telemarketing. Truly, getting fired that day, with my associated reaction, should be the getting fired template reaction for us all!

As I write this current page, my reaction to my firing still humors and amuses. I really should have been dismayed. But given all factors, I was otherwise pleasantly adjusted. So, I waited at my bus stop. I clearly remember while waiting for my route "52" bus, I remained amid an active and intense series of psychotic and delusional ideations. Others lingered next to me on the street. I remember, as we waited together, that life seemed to me like a play on a stage rather than a customary life feel. I remember some additional FBI ideations and once I boarded the bus I wondered what the other passengers would think of my supposed divine presence.

During the ride, my identity morphed back, from Jesus to Robert, but nevertheless God remained my cognitive copilot. I remember God speaking with me mostly concerning my spiritual allegiance to thee!

On the way I survived a series of further paranoid ideations of a most uncomfortable sort indeed. I thought God was intensely testing me while others were eager to persecute me. I finally reached my stop, and I reached the streets again. Upon exiting the bus, I felt a tremendous relief now away from others and their perceived malevolent projections.

It was dusk and the air was sweet. I had a few blocks to walk to get to my apartment. The sun was warm. During my walk, I continue to hear God talking to me and we had some of our usual discourse (this was certainly not my first psychotic ideation with God as a player). I was reflecting on my day as our dialogue maintained. About one block from my home, I queried God about my very hectic day including being fired and also being rampant with bothersome ideations. It was a long day indeed. For me, the day was akin to ten days and one.

"God?" I asked, "Why did you put me through such an experience and such an intense day?" God retorted, and this is verbatim as I clearly recall, "Because today is my tribute to Jimi Hendrix!"

I had not previously taken astute stock of the then cloudy dusk skies in my proximity but after God's comment my attention veered to above the horizon. In my eyes reflected a sublime shade of purple amid a cloudy haze. I then put two and two together. The skies were a product of God's immediate and prescient creativity and the then skies easily could have qualified by the title of "Purple Haze!" God informed me that his procreational skies were a tribute to Jimi Hendrix. The skies indeed were a shade of a most aesthetic purple haze, and I do attest, only God could have created such an artful skyline. I thought to myself; indeed, this is a true and exquisite render of a tribute to Jimi Hendrix!

God spoke to me at once regarding his ode and I immediately noticed the purple haze of the sky. The timing was pinpoint. The artful render could not have been more characteristic of such an ode. Once ago, when I had such routine dialogues with God, he was always awfully hard on me, but he also used to tell me he was so tough on me because he knew my strength and my faith; otherwise, he wouldn't be so powerful to my perceptions. I often thought my then relationship with God was like that of "Job" from the Bible. God was very tough on me, but he knew I would not lose my abiding faith.

Just prior to God's announcement regarding his "Tribute to Jimi Hendrix," I asked God the purpose and the why's of my ever so hectic and difficult day. Just after my asking, God put it into immediate perspective. My day was long because it was God's daily plan of a tribute to Jimi Hendrix. Once I put two and two together, those being, God's words to my ears regarding his "Ode to Jimi" with the correlation of the purple haze of the celestial sky, my day indeed made perfect sense to my then intellect and senses. Indeed, my day was as it was because God was going to pay tribute to Jimi! With this connectivity, my arduous and most difficult day appeared with great clarity, congruence, and now profound meaning.

I was put to my paces because God's daily plan was an "Ode to Jimi Hendrix."

With this now ultra-clarified perspective and profound recognizance, at the moment it all coalesced and I had a most hearty self-laughter, and the comic relief abandoned the heavy weights on my shoulders. Little did I know, at the start of my day, would it end in "God's Tribute to Jimi Hendrix." This episode I will never forget. It was the perfect end to an unbelievable day. I will share with you; I could not make this up even if I wrote the greatest of all fiction.

Alas, now on my further nonfiction, did I ever tell you about my then ontological lobotomy? Allow me to now share on my lobotomy delusion as my nonfiction will again broach a sort of unfathomable fiction.

CHAPTER 4
MY ONTOLOGICAL LOBOTOMY

We once again jump into our mutual time machine and return to my mid-twenties. During this specific time, I am again amid a florid psychosis, non-compliant of medication, and neglect of engagement in formalized mental health care treatment. My psychosis worsened to the point, once again, where my mental illness was again obvious to my loved ones.

My family arranged an intervention of sorts. My mother, father, aunts, and uncles arrived at my apartment to address my acuity. They informed me of prior arrangements of theirs. They surrounded me, both in proximity and love, and told me they wanted to take me to a psychiatric hospital. I think they believed I would be reticent, or resistant, but I quickly agreed. But the reason I so quickly assented was because, at the time, I was experiencing a symptom clinically known as an "idea of reference." An idea of reference is a specific cognitive thinking error, and it can serve as a productive trigger.

An idea of reference is ascribing a personal meaning, or semiotic, to an otherwise benign environmental variable that in fact carries no such attributable semiotic. It often occurs in psychosis and often inflames psychosis as a certain trigger.

For example, let us say we are conversing, and you scratch your chin in a particular manner. If I was operationally psychotic and observed your gesture and I accordingly thought to myself, "He scratched that way because he wants me to know he hates me." This would be ascribing a sort of meaning to an otherwise uncorrelated environmental variable.

"He scratched his chin because he wants me to go to hell."

This is another example of an idea of reference. We with schizophrenia, oftentimes, mis-attribute otherwise benign variables and assign malevolent motive. Ideas of reference often trigger and flourish amid a florid psychosis. They operate according to our misattribution. When they are prominent, our interpretation of reality becomes, in a most general and global ontological perspective, entirely misinterpreted, and hence, psychotic. Indeed, he scratched his chin. Likely, however, in reality, he had a scratch!

When my family arrived at my humble dwelling this day, and when they said they wanted to hospitalize me, I quickly assented because internally I ascribed an entirely different meaning to their intervention. Exclusive to the reality of taking me to the hospital, I thought my family wanted to show my then perceived delusional fame to others by driving me in the car for others to see. I was amid the delusion of being famous, or more succinctly, infamous. At the time, I thought everybody on Earth knew who I was and, as such, it triggered in me ample paranoia and psychosis.

The story of how I arrived at this specific delusional cognitive status is another story, of another sort, and of another discrete episode. The rub for our intent now, however, is I quickly assented to the hospital because I thought I was going to be publicly paraded, and at the very moment of my assent, I was agreeable to a perceived parade!

We are now capably on course to the hospital and to my perceived lobotomy. We drove 45 minutes to the hospital, and I got settled in. It was an upscale hospital thought to be the best in my locale. I have my family to thank for this particular investment.

Amid my two-week admission, I started on a new medication to me called Clozapine. Some seven days after starting the Clozapine I was discharged home because I once again was lucid, and the change in my mental status was a most remarkable turnaround. My newfound clarity was astounding to all!

But before the coda comes the prelude. We now delve into the delusional episode I comically title "My Lobotomy!"

I remember getting acclimated to the unit. The first day I was there I played video games by myself and made microwave popcorn. The hospital was like a posh hotel, and it had all the amenities. It was a campus. It had individual cabanas serving as units for various mental health populations. It also had a dining hall, amazing at that, and I put on some 10 needed pounds. In my cabana environment were twenty peers, and of course sets of mental health providers including from shift to shift. I tell you, the food at the dining hall was exquisite!

I remember chewing on my popcorn while playing video games. I also remember sitting back and watching an NBA (National Basketball Association) finals game. At the time, and I find this now most comical, I was substantially unaware of the greater whole. Rather than feeling hospitalized, I felt like I was on a vacation. Of course, such a low stress environment is exactly what I needed because high stress can significantly affect mental health especially someone in an active psychosis. This vacation felt conducive for me to relax; nevertheless, if I were in a lucid state of mind, I would've been at least concerned if not downright significantly troubled by my then current situation. I remember, for a night or two, I did not seem to have a care in the world as I absorbed the hospital's luxuries. Again, I have my dear family to thank for absorbing the expense. I was very fortunate and this I know!

I was ushered into a single room near the nurse's station. It was nighttime and I laid down eyes wide open listening to the quieter nighttime ambiance bereft of all the daytime hustle and bustle between patients and staff. I lay in my bed, and I remember it so clearly. I drifted off into a light sleep. When you are in a psychiatric hospital staff rounds are routine and around the clock. Every fifteen minutes a staff person checks all the patients for reasons of decorum and safety. So, as I try to doze, every fifteen minutes the door cracks open and a dutiful staff member observes the room and me for reasons of safety and just good, generalized care. But it's difficult to sleep when you know every fifteen minutes someone will be opening the door, exposing an unwanted sliver of light, and checking on my safety. But again, it's good care and good protocol. It does not entice sleep so much but nevertheless it's required. As an aside, some ten years later, I was the staff checking on others every fifteen minutes when I worked in a psychiatric crisis unit. I have been on both sides.

I fell asleep, and a light one at that. Yes, every fifteen minutes the door opens, and someone looks at me and it's a little unnerving. I sleep lightly over the course of the next six hours half aware of the routine fifteen-minute checks. I remember explicitly the face of the gentleman who was the night staff observer. If I could draw, according to my memory, I could sketch the face. I remember I woke up around six am.

When I wake up, two cognitive items are prominent.

The first is an unsettling ideation now known to me as then delusional. I have a notion that while I was sleeping, without my cognizance nor consent, I was removed from my bed, lobotomized, and then returned to my bed. I find myself amid a false belief that I was lobotomized. I lay in my bed paranoid and delusional. In retrospect, it was dream induced secondary to the routine fifteen-minute checks. But there I lay, now believing I was lobotomized and my mind races.

The second cognitive item of my awareness, specifically regarding my room environment, is a sort of sterile characteristic. I gaze about my room, amid belief of an overnight lobotomy, and my perception abides according to a sense of medical sterility. My room appears to me unusually white, whiter than any norm, and unusually and impeccably void of any extraneous objects and with a feeling of an ultra-sort of minimization. There is nothing in my room beyond a few items of pragmatic function. My room feels similar to a medical operating room, or the feel of the like of being in a dental chair as the technician removes the dental instruments from the sterile plastic bag. The combination of the sense of sterility, whiteness, and the occupying belief of being lobotomized all support and reinforce each other creating a most novel and odd perceptive gestalt.

I absorb the consequences. I lay thinking about this newest ontological predicament. Of course, a paranoia swells as well, but for some unknown reason, the unwarranted belief is only subtle and not enthusiastic. Thankfully, for whatever latent and unknown cognitive protective factor, the paranoia is not gripping and my emotional state and is largely and mostly unaffected. Mostly, I am only a touch concerned but the panic alarm, again, for some unknown reason, is not blaring or typically obnoxious. I lay concerned, but only a tad.

There I lay. My perception is of a white sterility and my belief is a recent lobotomy. I am alone in my room and alone in my thoughts. It is early morning, around six am. The sun is shining now slightly through the window. I begin to weigh the variables and my coping means begin to activate. Prior to this moment, it is of importance to note that prior to this episode I had previously been through troves and troves of very disturbing psychotic episodes. This was not my first episodic rodeo!

With all the psychotic trauma in my learned back pocket, my current situation does not overwhelm me. To me, at this moment in this particular episode, I remain unexpectedly calm and shall I say emotionally centered. There must be a reason I am largely at ease, although to this day, I still cannot fathom why I did not jump from my skin amid yet another sort of panic. But, indeed, I did not and largely I was emotionally unaffected, that is thanks being, to an unidentified form of a most helpful and perhaps external grace. I take a few minutes to process my predicament and I approach a resolution.

I think to myself,

"Robert, you were just lobotomized. This is not a good thing. Well, maybe it'll help. Things cannot be worse!"

I suppose in a way and in my own mind, I was heralding the stigmatized lobotomy and was psychologically inclined towards a beneficiary. Then I thought, "Now what?" I seek an action plan at this early morning hour. I thought "Now what should I do?" I kid you not, amid this ostensible reckoning and disturbing predicament ripe with malevolent semiotics in waiting, and amid a reasonable appraisal of potential great doom and despair, my answer in formulation to a strategic action plan beheld of this lasting wisdom, insight, and transcendent ideation by accordance to this conclusion:

"Well, I guess I should go to breakfast."

I indeed stood tall from the supine, took a shower, got dressed, and headed with my peer group to the adjacent dining hall. My action plan was on target, indeed, because amid the day's activity the delusion receded, and its veracity diminished and then fell extinct. To this day, I remember the details of this episode and I now find its conclusion, that being heading to "breakfast," as not only hysterically comical given the potential crisis but also sage in its banal ways. I suppose the moral to this particular episode resides as if ever status post a lobotomy, remember a hearty breakfast will assuage. I'm telling you; you can't make this stuff up!

CHAPTER 5
I CONTROL THE ECONOMY AND "DEER HEART"

Together again, we board our efficient time capsule. But prior to boarding, I retort, "Did I ever tell you about the six months when I was in charge of the US economy?" Of course, I offer with a wink, but the question preludes our next episodic delusion and I again offer "You can't make this stuff up!"

We jump into our travel time machine, and we arrive in my mid 20's, some 24 years inherent to my bones. I am again amid an unmedicated psychosis.

This next episode lasted me for a long time, some six months, and its theme came with many variations. For six months, I toiled with this delusion, and I must admit this thematic delusion was arduous; but, like the rest of my episodes, given a temporal distance and perspective, its humor abides.

Did you hear that voice? But before launching into certain voices with associated proper names, I must offer a disclaimer. This episode includes then President Bill Clinton. He does not know me, he has never seen me, and he does not know I exist. His involvement is purely according to my then delusional content. I now assuredly know I never crossed paths with President Clinton and the following episode is entirely and purely delusional. As such, my disclaimer is completed, and its coda achieved.

In the middle of a onetime rational mental faculty, little by little, I submerged amid psychotic waters. I began to hear the voice of the then

President William Clinton, also known as Bill Clinton. I began to hear his voice from the external environment mostly emanating from the skies above. His voice's source, I perceived, came associated with a government satellite technology that allowed the government to watch me from the skies and often times President Clinton's voice pierced the clouds directly to my ears!

Allow me to clinically recapitulate for a moment.

What indeed is going on from a clinical perspective? Well, as always common to the psychosis germane, a conglomeration is amidst. I am experiencing auditory hallucinations. These voices contribute to my growing belief, then a full belief and according to delusion, of being surveilled by the government via some sophisticated sort of obsequious technology to further governmental initiative. My associated moods can be found with some range given the duration and offshoot variables to this delusion. Amid this delusion, I am variably paranoid, persecuted, overwhelmed, irritable, and oftentimes scared.

I tangent for a moment to reflect on a relevant schizophrenia symbiosis. In schizophrenia, delusions about the government are common. I find it most intriguing and fascinating in our delusional similarities and at times our mutual commonness. I wonder why this is so. I wager such an etiology resides in a common brain organicity and for me this explanation suffices and informs. I suppose a brain can only malfunction in a finite number, and hence, common cognitive deficit equals common phenomenology. Nevertheless, such a commonness always piques and intrigues my comprehension.

The serendipitous aside, let us return to the spot. It is proper now to take about a six-month temporal perspective to this episodic delusion. Allow me to dissect this "government surveillance" delusion a bit further. My life becomes thoroughly occupied according to this persistent delusion. Sometimes the voices go extinct for the moment, and I feel in the clear from the surveillance. But, inevitably, the governmental shouts from the skies ensue once again. President Bill Clinton's voice is prominent to my delusion. However, I hear other voices too.

This fallacy plays like a sonata.

It strikes all sorts of delusional chords. Firstly, I try to figure out why I am being surveilled. After a temporal toil amid this psychosis, I conclude my governmental nemesis abides according to the pure happenstance of simply being the "chosen one," and for no other reason. I simply was picked, according to luck and more specifically my bad luck, to parlay certain governmental initiatives. It therefore begs, what were these initiatives?

To my mind, the government is making me famous to all living on Earth. The government is broadcasting my presence to the entire global population inclusive to all others being able to visualize me and hear my thoughts verbatim. With this now constituted as my ground, I believe everywhere I go that everyone knows who I am, and they also know I am the most unfortunate "chosen one" by the government for its initiatives. Secondary to my perception, others in my environment are always delighted by my presence because I am the most unfortunate chosen one to the exquisite delight of all others. This "chosen" quality is a certain governmental initiative in favor of the rest of the population who can delight by their own avoidance to my own harrowing predicament. Of course, learning to deal with this "chosen" aspect takes acclimation.

At times, I feel hopeless and scared out of my socks! But after months, I psychologically integrated to a degree, but I still hate it and passionately do so!

Then ensues another government initiative. The government has decided my behavior will help control the economy.

How so? I will be an economy guinea pig of sorts. While amid the government surveying me, any products I purchase, or only plainly see with my eyes, will be the products that are highlighted by the government in its capacity for economic promotion.

If I touch an eclair, for example, the dessert will get economic governmental attention. If I see a national chain business in passing, it gets its further due. Another aspect to my "control" of the economy ensues through my TV. When my TV is on, mind you I am alone just watching TV, I am amid the belief that every product I deliberately blink at, while watching TV, again gets national play within the government's product promotion. If I blink at a Jaguar, the car gets national economic support. If I blink at a whopper, Burger King gets props. Everything I see, or touch, or purchase gets an enhanced promotion.

I believe in its procedure because each new day and each passing hour finds me among differentiated goods and services. In other words, I touch on a full spectrum of products and so most all will gain their due depending on my correlated activity. My "control" of the economy also has bearing on the daily stock market and I find myself now serendipitously interested in the stock market, and to the greater economics. As I drive about, or pass time in my dwelling, I am of the belief that all my behaviors and sightings help motor the general economy. I am most convinced. This delusion rumbles in my mind for a robust six months. From its offshoot, then ensues its related delusion I now refer to as "Deer Heart."

You know, being in control of the US economy comes with associated stress!

Further, being constantly surveilled by the government also reigns with associated stress. For months I felt ogled and constantly so. Under such a felt microscope, my moods began to primarily point to paranoia and persecution. In no manner or way did I want this persistent and unrelenting surveillance. It drained my emotional aquifer.

Based on not wanting this attention, I am sure you might understandably concur, I became emotionally vexed. My feelings of paranoia and persecution crescendo. I simply could not allude, avoid, or shake off the perceived surveillance attention. At the time, I was not driving and so I took public transportation or walked to all places. I would take the bus to go to the mall or walk to the nearby pizza shop. As I went about my day, again, everywhere I went I believed everyone knew who I was, that is, the unfortunate "chosen one." This confluence ramped up my emotions and terribly so!

Now enter my delusion self-titled, "Deer Heart!" In my current psychotic state, allow me to iterate, I was amid the delusional belief of the availability of mind-to-mind communication. This misbelief of telepathy is, again, believing one can dialogue with others solely via thought and without need for spoken word. The rub being, everywhere I went I believed in a mutual sort of dialogue without the need for actual expressed verbalizations.

This dialogue was inclusive of all the people in my environment, that is, in addition to the government voices and other extraneous voices I was experiencing including across vast geographies. Oftentimes, given this intensely stressful gestalt, my fear reactions would initiate, and my heart rate would increase due to the fearful adrenaline surge supported by my intense feelings of persecution.

Little by little, I began hearing the name "Deer Heart." Slowly and incrementally, the name became synonymous with my own. Rather than calling me "Robert," little by little I believed others, via mind-to-mind communication, began to call me "Deer Heart." "Why as such?" I initially pondered.

Well, soon the answer clarified. I was being called "Deer Heart" because, in the presence of others, my heart was beating so rapidly, due to my stress, that others were mocking me for my obvious and illustrative somatic fear. The semiotic became clear to me. A deer's heart, I figured, beats rapidly as compared to the human. They were comparing my elevated heart rate with the rapid heart rate of a deer. They called me "Deer Heart." For weeks on end, I heard people referring to me as such. Every time I was fearful came its reverbiage and its attached badge. Conversely, the verbiage would also primarily trigger my fear and anxiety.

The following was the episodic delusion of how I was instrumental to the economy with the combination of the tag name,

"Deer Heart."

As I now reflect on this effervescent, abundant, and overflowing episode, and as I now pen amid the luxury of my warm and comforting apartment, this episode ably feathers my right arm funny bone, and it does so with a satisfying intellectual congruence. It bothers me not. It humors me so. From instigating the economy to my re-branding known as "Deer Heart," I again attest, you just cannot make this stuff up. Nonfiction again is indeed stranger than a most fictional sort of fabrication.

CHAPTER 6
MY DISH-WASHING EXTRAVAGANZA AND WHERE TO HIDE!

For this occasion, we now again climb aboard our time travel vehicle and zoom backwards in time to my age 25, or approximately therein.

I am non-compliant in my mental health treatment. At this point, my denial yet reigns as I again am sloughing off and neglecting to take my prescribed medications (that is, Zyprexa 10mg, twice daily). We arrive, circa 1996, at a most quaint and hospitable Greek-Italian restaurant. Here, you will find me as the 40 hour per week dishwasher. I attest, this entails a lot of dishes.

I am working as a dishwasher for two primary reasons with a third add-on. First, I need to pay the rent. Second, I needed a job at once. Lastly, I am still trying to find myself vocationally in the bigger picture and this culinary experience allows me to tread water for the time being. Overall, I washed dishes for 18 months. I do declare, status post my dish-washing experience, I forever hold those in similar position as a most noble sort of occupation, that is, when you think of its full consequences.

Most restaurant dishwashers, as did I, along with knocking out the dishes additionally help in the greater culinary prep (i.e., salads and the sort), clean from top to bottom, serve as a gofer on occasion as needed, run ice to the bar, and singularly close the kitchen for the night. It is pure noble manual labor. I am glad of its experience despite being amid my then ever flourishing psychosis.

Over the course of these 18 months, each day came with a brand-new episodic delusion or at least a continuance of a delusion from the day's prior. I was mostly floridly psychotic. But, to my credit, I did the job, was reliable, and I suppose I filled a chronic restaurant need (kitchen help). Beyond the character I built doing this noble job, my hands for the longest while appeared as wrinkled prunes because they were constantly immersed in the washing waters. It is interesting how some vocations leave evidence in one's hands!

As the restaurant dishwasher, I had a really great relationship with the married couple who were its owners. They treated me well, almost like a family member. In addition to my paycheck, every so often the owner would kick me a twenty spot and tell me he was thankful for my work. All in all, I liked the work. The concurrent florid psychosis, however, was not so favorable. While working in this position at least one hundred delusional tales followed but allow me to share a few of the most memorable. Upon retrospection, many such tales now abide with a tincture and timbre of humor and increasingly so as time yet further passes.

Firstly, I will share a few minor episodes as preludes to the then ultimate crescendo personally and affectionately remembered and self-titled as "Where to Hide." But before we get to the delusion of that please allow me some misconception openers. The former will be briefer and the coda in more detail.

Some eight months into my employment and secondary to a delusional underpinning, I feel compelled to take the shoelaces out of my sneakers and walk about with my sneaker tongues flapping about. I don't specifically recall the ideation behind the behavior, but I am most sure I came across as wildly eccentric, if not outright psychotic. I traversed about, in the kitchen as such, for some couple of hours. Psychotic behavior, for sure, but benign enough.

During my dish-washing vocational I happened to be interested in horse racing. I live proximate to a well-known horse racing track.

I remember while amid my duties, one fine day, I turned the radio channel in the kitchen from soothing oldies to the horse racing network. Thoroughbred racing was active, and I abruptly made an announcement to the entire kitchen regarding the upcoming race. I drew everyone's attention to the race and insisted everyone choose a horse for some good fun! I took note of everyone's choice prior to the race. The race began and the horses were off, and will you know it, for the next two minutes the kitchen came to a standstill as everyone goaded their selection. The entire staff, and the owners too, ceased their activity and rooted on their chosen horse! Only someone half out of their mind, as was I, would orchestrate such goings-on. But indeed, I did. According to his choice, the prep cook won the race. I remember the horse's name was "Perfect Execution." Again, this instigation was constructive of my cognitive psychosis.

The behavior benign enough. No harm, no foul.

Another dawn passes and a new day plays again in the kitchen. Upon my entrance, I began the day like most with a fair degree of tabula rasa. The day began with zero expectation of what would follow on this most very bizarre of days. As customary, I can be found replenishing relevant restaurant supplies i.e., silverware, dishes, and bar items. Additionally, and often so, my hands remain capably submerged in hot waters scrubbing kitchen accessories. Per usual, I too am frequently bent into the large water basins scrubbing and cleaning with an aid from Brillo.

Amid my duties begins another episodic delusion provoked within the confines of the Greek-Italian restaurant. My first delusion enters my psychological space. I can be found again amid self-deception on the ability of telepathic communication i.e., communication with those in the restaurant via mind-to-mind without need for overt verbalizations. According to this delusion, without me uttering any words, I again feel I am amid an ample "discourse" with others only it is without need for spoken word. Amid this misconception, after several hours of labor, my perceptions morph into another sort of novel ontology. I begin to view my mind, and the minds of others, as a sort of material object i.e., like a perceived tangible dot, or a dash, or a small line.

This "dot," pragmatic for our comprehension, seems to me like a material object similar to a pot or pan only smaller and of a different shape. This material representation, in my mind, begins to signify to my observing ego as my innate "soul." The minds of others take the same material form including by appearance of a sort of material object also presenting as a sort of dot. In the end, it feels like my soul is a dot and so too the souls of others appear to me as dots. Add in the deluding of mind-to-mind communication, or be it now, soul to soul communication, and it appears to me that dot to dot communication is verace. Again, this dot-to-dot communication is playing out in my mind without need for any requisite overt verbalizations.

My perceptions are now convinced, and duped, regarding the capacity for all the kitchen players to be able to communicate soul to soul. I am amid the perception of an abundant discourse with all those in my environment, but it just ontologically follows without perceived need for any speaking. Then follows the big circus! My perceptions turn ever sour and more malevolent. I begin to perceive the souls of all the rest present in the kitchen beginning to collude. The other collective souls together now seek my persecution, and a circus amid the Big Top ensues. I begin to perceive, in my mind's eye, that their dots i.e., their souls are now chasing my dot i.e., my soul and are attempting in some manner to persecute my soul by manner of a type of soul capture. I begin to perceive that their collective souls are chasing my single soul about the locale, that being, the kitchen. Feeling I am chased about, I begin to try to "hide" my soul in the whereabouts of the kitchen. I begin to look about the kitchen for my soul's hiding spot. I found a nook but soon they pinpointed it. I found another kitchen nook and they identified my locale again. I continue to look for hiding spots and for a while, the result is better than others. This game of chase unfolds as a procedural delusion over the course of the next several hours.

I have an inspiration.

Creativity strikes and I think out of the box. I conjure hiding my soul outdoors on the top of the exterior restaurant signage. "They will never find me here," I think, as I have now absconded from the proximate geographic territory. I perceive my soul perched like a bird on the exterior restaurant sign. Here, I think, I have found a capable respite. But after a few minutes, I perceived a self-induced error. I perceive that a noise emanates from my soul while perched, and as such, it audibly triggers my reconnaissance again to the collective others. I again frantically seek a new hiding.

I remain often hunched over in my dish pan waters washing pots, pans, and silver. In my mind, I am frenetically plotting to find a place for my soul that will be safe from the chase! I am in survival mode, and I am seeking salvage and refuge.

Up to this point, this delusion is wrought with fear as I perceive myself to be under a stern attack. My mind spins seeking hiding amid the material locales in my immediate environment. My eyes gaze about looking for safe placing. I again then conjure a new alternative. For its greater clarity, however, I must share prior to this new creative spark, I was pruning to God for assistance given my perceived peril. Because of my longings and extensions to the Almighty for help, my mind is circling about the spiritual.

A new idea rings like a bell to my mind and my ears receive. I have a new notion as to the perfect hiding spot. I think to myself rather than hiding amid the material, I should hide amid the more ambiguous and immaterial. Eureka! My new hiding exists within the lines of a poem. Additionally, my refuge rests in a specific poem well familiar to me.

When I was a child, I was taught the following little ditty of a poem by my dad. Its lines follow as such: "Here's the church, here's the steeple, open it up and here are all the people." In addition to its prose and along with speaking the lines, my dad showed me an associated brief gesticulation with both my hands that correlated to the poem's spoken prose. It is amid this literary prose, along with a perceived sort of spiritual occupancy within my hand's gesticulations, that I indeed find my ultimate hiding spot.

Once conjured, I then implement. Remarkably, all the voices in my head and related psychotic discourse suddenly quiet and strikingly so. With this vibrant new idea comes an associated quieting in my mind and, for the moment, my psychotic content quells. I am no longer hearing voices and life once again takes a more rational perspective absent of the frenzied psychotic content. Like a light switch, with my new idea, my mind immediately quiets and the psychosis, for the time being, is capably discouraged.

I finished the night's work. A certain lucidness has returned but fear yet lingers at the fringes of my mind. In retrospect, my solution to finding the perfect hiding locale seems to me surely inventive. Please remember if you ever need a place to hide a poem may indeed well-suit. Surely, if one was looking for you or me, occupancy in a poem further obfuscated by an associated hand gesture, I assume to be a most difficult finger. Who knew solace and refuge could be found amid a poem's dwelling?

In temporal retrospect, my solution of hiding in a poem ably bemuses my senses, tickles my right humerus elbow, and when given my right disposition can induce in me a most hearty guffaw along with a most proper roll of the eyes, that is, now all in good spirits. I could not make this up even if I were the craftiest of all fiction writers.

Lastly, allow me to briefly capitulate on this psychotic experience from a clinical psychological perspective for some greater comprehension.

The symptom conglomeration assumes by the presence of the mind-to-mind communication delusional belief, along with the presence of auditory hallucinations, and tied in a bow by perceptions and feelings of paranoia and persecution. The clinical remedy relies in understanding the delusion as such, via improved reality-testing, recognizing intellectually the ontology of the auditory hallucinations, and having a mindful awareness of the associated moods as triggered. Accordingly, such psychotic content can be ameliorated via several portals of intervention.

At this point in my life, now living with schizophrenia for so long, such a delusional episode would have no such persuasion or significant cognitive occupancy. But like all of us, we live and learn, and move on. Incidentally, speaking of moving on, did I happen to ever tell you regarding my experience of another sort of supreme and remarkable divine intervention? We now angle in its direction.

42

CHAPTER 7
GOD, HEAVEN ON EARTH, AND PIZZA

I am unmedicated (medication non-compliant) and not actively engaged in any ongoing mental health treatment. I am status post, and well beyond, my formalized diagnosis of schizophrenia but I am again in avoidance of my suggested medications. At this very current moment, I now know with certitude, for me, it follows no medications equals active and recurring psychosis. However, it was a learning curve for me to arrive at such a conclusion.

Many years ago, I could be found supine on my bed as nested in my studio apartment. The apartment is tiny, but I find it cozy for my own needs. I lay in bed and my mind is racing. It is afternoon. My psychosis is hitting all its buttons including my wrestling with feelings of paranoia and persecution. At this time, you will find me amid persecutory delusions with associated persecutory auditory hallucinations. I remember, at this very point, my psychosis was capably fatiguing me, and I was incredibly stressed.

I lay in bed trying to make sense of my misunderstanding and troublesome psychosis. I am amid the delusion that the world population, every single person, and soul included, along with the Almighty God, are amid motive to persecute me. Amid my delusional status, we together again arrive with active ideational God content. Such religious-type ideations are common among us with schizophrenia, and I am again in its throes.

To reiterate, I share not on God content for any sort of persuasion or admonishment simply as parcel to my then ontology.

43

Such belief or non-belief in God I find a most personal matter of choice, and correspondingly, without any need of my intrusion. Nevertheless, God plays the lead role in this particular episodic psychosis.

I was wrestling with my acute cognitive torment. I am diligently trying to problem-solve as to why all subjects in the universe are colluding in my persecution and associated social isolation.

I am amid the belief that all in the world are against me and including God too! From such a vantage, where is any solace?

In addition to the persecutory delusions and persecutory auditory hallucinations, I am also amid the delusion, again, of the availability of mind-to-mind communication, that is, the ability to communicate with others (and God) without need for spoken words and also capable across spatial geography. This psychotic conglomeration again unfolds to my observing mind like a play on a stage.

The last presenting psychotic ingredient, specific to this episode, includes the cognitive distortion known as "spotlighting." Spotlighting is the erroneous belief that one is the center of attention in regard to one's felt presence in the greater social environment. When spotlighting is active, in relation to others, you feel as though you are wholly and entirely the center of social attention inclusive not to compliment but rather to a collusive conjoined malevolence.

Characteristically, I consequently feel socially isolated from all the rest, that is, God and entire populace included. When spotlighting is active, I think all such other entities are together delighting in my persecution and are enjoying my great adverse predicament.

"Why? Why is this happening?"

I ardently wrestle with my imposed perceptive torment and slow torture. As I wrestle with my psychosis amid my "why me-isms?" my cognitive-behavioral emotional state is atrocious. I lay supine on my bed fighting my demons! During this time, my cognitions and my moods are full-tilt dystonic. I am in psychological darkness. I am in my psychological forest. I hope for relenting illumination, but it yet vigorously evades. Primarily, at this moment in my psychotic sequela, a small sliver of hope yet remains as I intellectually search for relief, absolving, and solution. Hopelessness fast approaches yet has no full occupancy.

I pour over the variables of my uncomfortable gestalt. How's, why's, solution-seeking, and means of escape enthusiastically churn in my mind. I feel like a solution avails, but I just cannot put my finger on its hidden pulse. I rummage through the contents of my mind seeking answers and solace. I am highly dystonic but not yet fully oppressed. Make no mistake, however, I am exhausted, and I feel entirely persecuted. I feel, however, a solution can yet be invented or found.

Did you hear that snap of the finger? Just like that, in the snap of a finger, abject adversity transmutes to sublimity. In an abrupt and sudden moment, the divine voice of God penetrates my darkness like an ardent ray of light. I will never forget this very moment and instant, including by its remarkable suddenness, when all my distorted feelings instantaneously upended, reversed, and capably turned sublime. As I once laid in torment, and just prior to this immediacy, I was amid a personal plea to God asking for a relieving reprieve. "Why are you putting me through this?" I asked of God amid my internal discourse. "Why?" Then in a moment of unequaled acuity, God's voice psychologically pierced and retorted, and this is verbatim, "Because I wanted to show you heaven on Earth!"

Unlike my previous experienced verbalizations from God, God's voice evaded the persecutory and otherwise was experienced as entirely syntonic, welcoming, and congruent. Fortuitously, I now receive his voice as powerfully inspiring, uplifting, and supportive. My sought solution has become wholly and certainly satisfied.

Can life change in an instant? In my experience, it can. This is why I always view hope as essential.

Without hope, we have extraordinarily little if not anything. In this instance, God indicates to me he put me through my druthers because, as verbatim again, "I wanted to show you heaven on Earth." Miraculously, my forlorn suffering now comes with purpose, and I am lifted from its throes. Conversely, I am now amid sublimity, that being, momentously and precisely following this heard proclamation from God.

I do not exaggerate, nor in the least, the next thirty minutes or so were the most sublime and peaceful of my entire life, hands-down and case fully closed! Amid God's perceived support and urging, I stand from my supine physical and emotional wrestle and take restorative deep breaths. In the full course of my life, I have never felt better! All shreds of darkness have evaporated, and I literally and figuratively now stand in a perceived wholesome light.

By a most startling fashion, my entire psychology has transmuted from pole to pole, and a momentous radically oppositional sort of welcome ontology ensues. I feel akin to a phoenix rising from the ashes. I hear God's voice speaking to me. I am now amid a sense of inspiration and motivation, and I decided to go for a walk outdoors with my destination being my hometown downtown area. I leave my apartment with miraculous optimism, wholesome congruence, and an overflowing internal peace and power.

I descend the stairs and make it to the street. I marvel at my abrupt ontological reversal. I feel terrific, inspired, and renewed. Amid these very moments, God feels abidingly as my copilot, yet indeed my guiding pilot! According to my senses, God's voice is thoroughly benevolent and is intimately amid my internal discourse. I feel directly connected with God's presence and voice. He is felt intimately within, and all my perceptions now reside with an abundant, overflowing, and congruent ontological benevolence. The shift in my psychological poles is utterly astounding. In recollection, I marvel.

My perceptions for the next thirty minutes are sublime, and this handful of minutes remains the most spectacular of my life, be it abiding psychosis aside. I tell you, my perceptions now feel warmly novel. My perceptions are accompanied by a tincture of a most peaceful and welcoming shade of an easy yellow. My vision feels sharp and clarified. As I descend the stairs and reach the street, God now begins an intimate conversation with me. I have never had such a benevolent sort of experience, and this abides to this very modern day and this very present moment.

I feel so at peace.

My perceived dialogue with God ensues. I begin walking the street heading to my downtown destination. I pass the post office with a deeply peaceful and warm ontology. As I gaze about at my remote scenery my perceived interaction unfolds. Each environmental object, person, place, or thing I observe then comes accompanied by an explanation from God as to why things are as such. Everything I look at God explains, and the clarity is entirely comprehensible and astounding. As I walk the street, God explains with a deep sense of love and astute clarity the purpose behind all things to which I am directly observing. If I look at a tree, then follows its explanation.

When I gaze at a building, another clarified explanation. I remain filled with warmth, extraordinary peace, and a never before sense of intellectual congruence. My perceptions continue to abide according to a most warming timbre of an easy yellowish tinge. Everything and all I see or observe, God perfectly explains to me as to its reason and purpose, and all such explanations qualify as abundantly benevolent. I am at peace with the universe. I feel a depth of understanding never experienced. Mostly, at this point as a further walk, I find myself seeing and then hearing God's voice and explanations. My own internal voice has quieted.

Fifteen minutes into my walk, I arrive at my destination. I decided to duck into my favorite pizza place for a bite. God stays with me. I entered the shop amid the best experience of my life! God's explanations persist. I order my slice, pay the cost, and sit. God clarifies to my perceiving eyes on a few last tidings including final comments regarding my immediate environment. I sit at the very last booth facing north to the rest. I take a hearty bite and then another.

Suddenly, as instantaneously as it all began, the experience abruptly terminates and immediately disparages.

I feel an energy leave my body, mostly from my chest cavity, and I now feel empty of a once undeniable source. Its energy evacuates. God's voice is now gone and is no longer. I sit with my slice for a few minutes as I frenetically attempt to reassume my prior moments ontology. I robustly seek a reinstatement. Despite my yearnings of a reclamation, it assuredly evades, and escapes and the experience altogether conclude. I resumed amid my routine psychological struggles. Now I feel empty. I know the experience is over altogether. I resume amid my normative ontological status knowing this spectacular experiential anomaly is over, and unquestionably so.

Admittedly, by comparison, this episode qualifies as less comical (although not altogether) and resides as exquisitely sublime, and to this day, exceptionally so and singularly above all the rest.

This experience I will never forget. In retrospect, I can see myself in that back booth in the pizza shop attending to my slice. In my mind's eye, I can clearly recollect my status while amid the ideation versus the very moment it came to its coda. I can see myself concurrently amid the experience and immediately thereafter. When I now think of the great disparity regarding the amid versus the status post, in retrospect and extraneous to its unquestionable sublimity, I marvel at the remarkable ontological disparities. At once it was sublime then instantly again mundane.

Yet pertaining and inclined of the comical, to this current day, the then abrupt change in the course of these events capably maintains a subtle bemusement to my senses and intellect. The experiential disparity is by the way of the Grand Canyon and its ontological diversity to this day feathers my elbow with a guffaw and chuckle. I see myself status post the intense and sublime experience, finishing my slice and remains, and to this very moment it all yet provides greater amusement.

Who am I to quibble regarding such distinct ontological poles?!

The prominent clinical themes include that of a "delusion, marked by religiosity." Religious ideations, for some, are common in schizophrenia. I am also amid auditory hallucinations i.e., hearing the voice of God. Lastly, the experience can be categorized as "syntonic," that is, a dispositionally agreeable sort of experience and delusion.

The clinical remediation to this scenario includes and entails, prior to its given momentum and eventful sequela, a capacity to recognize, that indeed, my mind resides as religiously preoccupied and also the identification of hallucinating voices that have no such logical source. To capably make these cognitive identifications and remediations primarily, or while the experience was occurring, would be exemplary of an active and personal cognitive "insight" and a demonstrable ability to effectively self "reality-test." At the time of this occurrence, I had no such insight. If the same sequel ensued at this very moment such an ontology would never ensue or gain such a momentum. I live and I learn! Such an experience I qualify as psychotic, although sublime it was. I do not fuel any current fires by convincing myself of its veracity.

I leave it at an episodic delusion, and I move on. Speaking of moving on, shall we together again traverse amid an otherwise cumulative sort of shared "mish-mosh?!"

CHAPTER 8
RAPID FIRE MISH-MOSH

Let us one last time harken our retro time machine travel and again arrive to my mid-twenties. Here you will find me amid a rampant temporal psychosis running its challenging course. I again was medication non adherent, and I was not actively engaged in any formalized mental health treatment or support.

By manner of vocation and day, you will find me as a cake decorator at the local supermarket and according to evening I was a wandering and troubled soul.

Indeed, I worked for about a solid year as a chain store supermarket cake decorator. External to my psychosis, this vocational dalliance was a great combination of fun and creativity, and additionally, a tasty snack was unanimously at hand. To this day, I can lend a critical eye to all birthday cakes front and center. Truly, a most novel sort of skill.

In this chapter, I am going to alter it by form. So, I am going to offer more of a rapid-fire sort of approach regarding my then psychotic ideation's. The ideation's occurred while working in the supermarket and others during my free time amid the greater community. These ideation's I offer, too, abide by a thorough psychotic accordance. Rather than expounding on it, however, we now will regale more in particular ideation's, that being, more on singularities and specifics rather than thematic wholes. Nevertheless, many of these ideation's were also characteristically episodic and each occurring with some temporal variance.

Strangely, some time ago, I kept hearing the word "modicums." I am actively amid auditory hallucinations, and I hear others projecting the word "modicum" to my direction, mind, and my awareness. In addition to these auditory hallucinations, I am also amid the delusion (again) of mind-to-mind communication; that is, the ability to communicate with others directly mind-to-mind without need for spoken language. Interestingly and coincidentally, time prior to this specific auditory hallucination, I had no prior conscious cognizance of the semiotic or meaning of the word "modicum" and I persistently thought to myself it was just a conjured word I was hearing. According to Webster, however, a modicum, as defined, is a "small portion" or a "limited quantity."

I kept hearing the word modicum!

Then I began to hear others saying, "He's trying to use his modicum!" For a good long while, I was hearing this persistent auditory hallucination, but I was confused as to its meaning. Initially, the word rang as entirely unfamiliar. After a while of hearing the word, however, I then curiously looked up its definition and its meaning read, absorbed, and then appreciated as such. Nevertheless, the portrayed projected semiotic initially seemed nonsensical to me. Why would others say, "He is trying to use his modicum?" It just made me no sense.

Then another semiotic took over and a comprehension coalesced to my then turbulent mind. I deduced and concluded, others were calling my brain a "modicum" by way of a perceived persecutory projection with the sign that my brain was a "small" entity or "limited" capacity. Others were ridiculing my brain as a "modicum" i.e., a smaller entity compared to the brains and intellects of others.

This auditory hallucination persisted and became repeated and persistently heard over the course of several months.

The irony remains I had no recognizance of the word prior to its auditory intrusion. I never consciously held its comprehension.

How it seeped into my subconscious is still unknown. I find it a most peculiar happenstance. At this very moment, however, in retrospect, I find this psychotic ideation beyond a humorous tickle and more robustly hysterical! Although at the time it was most unwelcome and intrusive, I now find its coalescing and ontology of a most comical sort. My brain referred to as a "modicum!" Tellingly, you just can't make this stuff up. Please feel free to chuckle yourself as this one-time wound is now well healed.

Now, I offer another psychotic ideation. I woke up one fine day with a novel morning idea regarding abduction by aliens. It is funny, psychotic perceptions in a general sense often look and appeal as different than normative perceptions both according to associated sight and a sort of gut feel. This alien abduction idea was thoroughly of a perceived differentiated sort. I woke up in the morning with a startle and the alien abduction was eagerly percolating amid my senses. As I left my modest abode, this idea gained in its momentum and veracity. Things again looked strange and different than the normative. Things felt weird, or as they say in psychological clinic-speak "bizarre."

For the next 3 to 4 hours, I cavorted about the community accomplishing my errands and tasks. The ultimate content to this ideation, and how I then comprehended my situation and its associated ontology, as entailed, included the idea of while asleep, during my slumber, I was abducted. This ideation was indeed bizarre. I am not aware how it fabricated but its presence and veracity was provoked.

The ideation was immediately present and verace upon my morning awakening.

My comprehended gist, by way of conclusion included, aliens abducted me while I slept. Further, I believed I was transported off the Earth and brought to an otherwise alien planet. As I dallied about my day, for several hours, I felt I was on an entirely separate planet from Earth.

I thought the beings I was amongst were alien life-forms with the associated caveat, that being, the aliens presented by the ostensible appearance of human beings. They appeared human but underling thought to be alien. Under this human veneer, the aliens had an entirely different appearance. I thought the aliens had the capacity to take a human appearance despite their otherwise differentiated alien inherence.

For the rest of the afternoon, I was on another planet amongst aliens who just looked like humans. The aliens, I believed, also behaved like humans; therefore, to me, all social interactions appeared normative and akin to my routine Earthly interactions. I thought the alien form was underneath the human ostensible! This ideation lasted a good, long afternoon.

The funniest part of this ideation was how I resolved its associated intellectual implications. I thought to myself, if indeed I am on another planet with aliens shrouded in the human ostensible, both according to appearance and behavior, I then thought "What's the difference?" as related to my Earthly inherence. If life on the alien planet portrayed similarly to my Earthly ontology, then why should I care about the ultimate truth or veracity? If life all proceeded the same, why should I worry if indeed I was transported away?! I thought, "If life is comparable on both planets, why should I care?"

This was my conclusion!

For whatever reason such logic, at the given time, well sufficed and satisfied. It was persuasive enough to my intellect and I really had no great lingering anxieties on this ideation. There was a sort of serene intellectual congruence, again for some serendipitous reason, and its greater ideation did not significantly provoke my angst. I thought if life portrayed the same, what's the difference?

After a bunch of hours, because of my easy acceptance of this particular ideation, the ideation faded, and my perceptions morphed back into my normative Earthly ontology, and I then believed myself back among humans on our cozy planet Earth. I remember this afternoon ever so clearly and it will not ever be forgotten. At this very moment, upon its recollection, it tickles my right elbow with a feathery appeal, and it continues concordant with an ample bemusement.

The clinical explanation to this particular episode includes an active delusion, that being, identified as "bizarre" type. Because of the absence of any great correlated intellectual distress, the fallacy is characterized as "syntonic" i.e., otherwise agreeable to one's intellect. My associated mood can be labeled as clinically "euthymic;" that is, neutral and absent of acute emotional distress. At the time, I was not hearing voices so auditory hallucinations do not pertain. The clinical remediation to such a delusion would entail the process of reality-testing in furtherance of moving away from delusion to more evidenced-based rationality. If you are curious, I have never lent this delusion any further credence or veracity. It was a delusion, not actual, and with ease I leave it as such.

Sometimes I would work an entire day at the supermarket and merely utter two words. I was often overtly very quiet but not because I did not think I was not amid vigorous communication with others.

I dwelled for months amid the telepathic communication delusion, characteristically including, its capacity across vast geographies. Because of this one-time pervasive deception, I could go hours and hours without speaking with others although I believed I was otherwise amid heavy interactive dialogues. Sometimes others would comment that I was entirely quiet. I thought then that they were being sarcastic because I indeed thought I was highly communicative. In reality, I said almost nothing over the course of hours and even days. I have always admired the person of few words, but this was well beyond such terseness and was a prolific quietness.

When I think back to this particular ontology it chuckles and guffaws me much. How I kept my mouth altogether shut and quiet, for hours and days, was indeed a sort of prolific and exaggerated behavior. This extreme, in my recollection and to this very day, kindly bemuses. Indeed, for a time, I was a man of few words, if any at all!

Continuing this chapter theme of a rapid-fire mish-mosh, let's amp our efficiency and quantification up yet another notch.

Did I ever tell you of my experience of feeling I was under "remote control" by my unseen neighbor?

This delusion occurred for days. I felt as if my every move were manipulated and controlled, and I could not shake the ideation for days. Otherwise, together excelling further on, did I ever share on my self-titled delusion of "dropping down?"

Dropping down was another personal misconception where I was convinced others could "drop down" their intangible mind to any desired locale in their body. This ideation blossomed as a persecutory delusion of sorts because I believed I personally had no such ability. I believed that others, if so desired, could move their mind away from their head to any other part of their body i.e., anywhere from head to toe. In fact, in support of this delusion, I had personal perceptions that the minds of others indeed were no longer in their heads and were in other areas of their bodies. I spent days amid the perceptions that I was communicating with others whereby their mind entity was elsewhere than in their head proper. These beliefs were extremely bizarre and disturbing.

I offer one final rapid-fire mish-mosh delusion. I was convinced over weeks of reincarnation. Further, I had persistent ideations that it was a fait accompli that once I passed from my current life I would materialize again as a child in an Asian nation. For weeks, I believed that I was going to pass and reemerge as a child on another continent. This delusion was bizarre but capably syntonic. Nevertheless, its delusional capacity is portrayed for endurance.

I have now capitulated in sharing some of my experiences. Many others I leave as yet, at this time, unwritten and unstated; however, those I have shared provide a nice cross sample, I think. I share these episodes because I want to help. I want to help others living with schizophrenia and their families. I want others to believe in recovery, and gainful at that. One day, I am most sure, the treatment success with schizophrenia will elevate tenfold. Once in the future, I steadfastly believe when someone is diagnosed with schizophrenia the prognostic will be optimistic and thoroughly so! I also know in my gut, in our current situation and modernity, "recovery" too is entirely possible, that is, given ample psychoeducation, the requisite acquisitive coping skills, and the proper support and treatment. In attestation, I exclaim schizophrenia is a livable condition!

Lastly, now please join me in my epilogue for summary and further motive reveal. The epilogue may be my most important chapter. After all, summary is associated with pleasant resolution. Together we proceed for one last dance and dalliance.

HITHER ON TO THE EPILOGUE.

Early on in my struggles with schizophrenia, I went to hell and back, and then returned yet again and one more time. It was arduous and miserable. But how drastically things have changed for the better! I want others to know, assuredly, however dark, and insurmountable things may feel at the very moment please know when you persist things indeed will improve.

Let my hell be a shortcut to your belief in a substantial recovery.

I wrote this book for one personal compelling reason. I wrote it because I passionately and absolutely believe in recovery from schizophrenia. Further, I have faith in each of us with schizophrenia to live gainful and satisfying lives. Additionally, I will sleep better at night knowing that treatment providers to those with schizophrenia, too, share such an outlook and prognostic. My intent is to supply optimism, hope, and a deeper understanding as to the ontology of schizophrenia.

With greater understanding then can follow adaptive coping. Nevertheless, allow me this caveat. Your recovery may indeed look different than mine. Recovery is a global sort of concept with different variables to consider.

The common thread to recovery, however, is at least twofold. Recovery entails a form of stability with diminished acuities and/or crises. Second, recovery is a psychological introject. By this I mean that once someone living with schizophrenia can accept its render and its imposed sort of ontology and meet and greet its voraciousness with a sort of personal confidence, it follows that schizophrenia can be managed and personally handled.

The combination of an attitude marked by an epistemological knowing of its management conjoined with temporalities of a sort of cognitive-behavioral stability, that is, absent of recurring acuities or crises, to me earmark as the essential ingredients to gainful recovery. Further, if someone finds themselves amid a triggered acuity and nevertheless maintains self-confidence regarding their acute management, this then reinforces the twofold dynamic and again leads one forth to stability, and gainful at that.

I passionately believe in recovery. But I must add, recovery is not like the wave of a wand. Mostly, recovery is a process and not an event. Further, like all subject matters in life of importance, education is paramount. The longer I live with schizophrenia the more I understand it and, so, the better I often cope. For me, recovery was a certain learning curve, and its aperture continues to this very moment.

Regarding my greater education related to schizophrenia, I have come to realize that each and every symptom inclusive to schizophrenia comes with an associated form of solution. My learning curve has included such discoveries of these solutions. Be them delusions, auditory hallucinations, and/or disturbance of mood and affect, all abide by an associated sort of solution, either in whole, partially, or by piecemeal.

One's accumulated knowledge regarding schizophrenia I label and self-define as "insight." Insight becomes a primary motor to recovery, that is, in addition to the medicinal and excellent provisional mental health treatment providers and care (as may be required). Insight is my global push back to my psychosis. Psychosis may render, but my internal discourse mitigates. My internal dialogue focuses on my learned solutions to any availing acute symptoms. In my back pocket, I have my personal cachet of associated and accumulated solutions.

Similarly to my solution-focused psychological approach, I certainly and truly believe that others, too, can develop their own solutions and cachet of needed coping means. I passionately believe others too can find their answers and in promotion of stability and gaining a sense of recovery. Learning from one's experiences aids in remediation. I wrote this book so others can develop a self-confidence in one's ability to cope with this sometimes-devilish disease, and also to acquire an abiding optimism and a never wavering sense of hope.

Make no mistake, recovery, and stability, or be it, a homeostasis across decent and expansive temporalities, is achievable. I earnestly want others with schizophrenia to believe in their capacity for a rewarding life. In my mind, all pertinent life goals, the same goals we all share, are achievable despite schizophrenia. Again, however, your recovery may look a bit different than mine, or to another with schizophrenia. Like the rest of humanity, your goals and achievements may differ from others, and most likely so. Nevertheless, many pertinent and satisfying life aims and goals remain ever viable.

I am compelled to write these books about living with schizophrenia. This will be my fourth book on the topic. Regarding the specificity of this book, I am intellectually urged to share regarding my numerable psychotic episodes. Rather, I have had so many duping episodes I'd rather submit its quantity as innumerable!

I went into detail grouping some of my most personably memorable and favorable episodes. In regard to the delusional content,

I refer to each as an episode, or as an episodic delusion. Each episode read, most hopefully, like a fiction story.

I share how I solved the inherent symptomatology inclusive to the greater episode. Each account has come with an undeniably correlated solution, or be it, a combination of different sorts of related solutions. From learning about the intricacies involved in each mind trickery, I have gained the requisite coping skills. This conglomerate of skills now seeped into my intrapsychic reservoir, I deem as "insight." My insight involves every cranny of coping skill gleaned from living with schizophrenia over these many years.

Indeed, I have now lived with schizophrenia for 25+ years. I was hospitalized three times. I have been involved in mental health treatment and care also for 25+ years. I have taken the antipsychotic Clozapine for decades. At this point, I consider myself a "schizophrenia veteran" of sorts. I also graduated from the schizophrenia school of hard knocks, then followed by a master's from the schizophrenia school of arts and sciences! But again, I jest.

Professionally, I am an LCSW (Licensed Clinical Social Worker). I have undergraduate and graduate degrees. My master's in social work was obtained in 2006. Since 2006, I have toiled as a mental health talk-therapist, including in a variety of settings with a variety of populations.

I do attest, my degree in social work has been ever useful because it is highly marketable. For me, social work has served me well.

Please know, as waters gone by, I shared a few details of my all-time favorite delusional episodes. I shared, within each one, the inherent struggles, gut wrenching pains, absurdities, and comedies.

Yes, comedy!

Psychosis is not ostensibly funny especially when amid its grueling courses. In my case, however, once at a temporary safe distance from my actuated psychotic occurrence, I have some etiologically unknown personal congruence. I often find humor in gone-by episodes. I even refer to my all-time favorite delusions as my personal "classics." I often retort to self when thinking about a vanished episode, "Now that was a good one!" Oftentimes, I will then self-chuckle. I think to myself, these delusions are so sensational that humor occupies and binds to the at once trickeries of my mind, and more specifically, with related comedic timbres; that is, with correlated temporal goodbyes.

There are a lot of crossovers, in those with schizophrenia, with shared types of delusions. This being so is the reason I also wanted to share on how I solve this false belief conundrum. Many of my delusions will be similar to those of others, that is, by according theme. And with common themes, common solutions. Let us not need to re-create the wheel when it factors as redundancy. I hope the lessons and skills I learned in coping with my episodic deception may truncate the process for others.

Within each chapter I hoped to share a pragmatic psychoeducation, acquisitive coping skills, and some humor too. Regarding these episodes, you simply cannot make this stuff up! Such episodes portray, to me, with persistent wonder. From whence does this content emanate?! Additionally, those of us with schizophrenia, we share these wondrous themes. Truly, it's a sort of beautiful aesthetic, at least, to this observing mind.

I wrote this book because of a vigorous belief vis-à-vis those others living with schizophrenia. It is imperative for me to state, with an ever-intensifying passion, I truly believe in the concept of "recovery." I personally believe that those living with schizophrenia, absent anosognosia, can recover and lead the lives of their choosing.

Every symptom of schizophrenia comes with an associated solution. I mean every symptom! It is just a matter of identifying it along with associative coping means and ways. My goal as a schizophrenia advocate, is to help change the perception, to the degree that is needed, that the natural trajectory in the personal phenomenology of schizophrenia is that of recovery; that is, a gainful recovery at that. The glimmer in my eye you see is this normative re-framing. My hope being, in the future, those diagnosed with schizophrenia will think of it as a routine health issue with capable treatments and expected recoveries.

In the future, treatment providers, too, will also be found with such a recovery perspective and they too will be ever hopeful of great outcomes. It is because of my prevailing inherent belief in recovery that within each chapter, amid detailing my delusional episodes, I also share on the associated solutions. I reveal the clinical perspective regarding the shared phenomenology. Accordingly, my lived experience reflects and glimmers alongside the correlated clinical framing or phenomenon. By sharing both lived experience and its associated clinical framework, we arrive at comprehension.

Each perspective informs the other, mutually, and exclusively. It is my hope that readers of this book will leave its company with a similar belief to my own. Recovery is normative given the proper perspectives, solutions, and skills. One day, schizophrenia will be routine. I carry no doubt.

I hope you enjoyed reading this book. Look out for other books by me regarding this subject.

ABOUT THE AUTHOR

Robert Francis was diagnosed with schizophrenia in 1995. He earned a bachelor's degree in 1993 and a master's degree in social work in 2006. Robert has been practicing as a mental health talk therapist for more than 15 years. He is currently a licensed clinical social worker (LCSW). Regarding the topic of schizophrenia, Robert has authored two earlier books.

His first book is titled On Conquering Schizophrenia: From the Desk of a Therapist and Survivor and his second book is titled The Essential Schizophrenia Companion; With Foreword by Elyn R Saks, PhD, JD. Robert's passion is to help others with schizophrenia to recover, as he did, and to live full, satisfying, and hopeful lives. Customary to his style, Robert writes with a characteristic warmth, humor, and inimitable insight.